Classic
AMERICAN
Motorcycles

Classic
AMERICAN
Motorcycles

Written by John Carroll: Photography by Garry Stuart

CHARTWELL
BOOKS, INC.

Page 2: *Harley-Davidson was one of only two U.S. motorcycle manufacturers to survive in business beyond World War II. It modernized its engines to overhead valves away from the popular flathead of which this big twin is a thirties example.*

Page 3: *The Cyclone was a short lived and briefly successful motorcycle by Joerns Motor Manufacturing of St. Paul, Minnesota.*

Right: *A 1913 V-twin Pope motorcycle with the then innovative plunger rear suspension.*

Published in 1997 by
Chartwell Books, Inc.
A Division of Book Sales, Inc.
Raritan Center
114 Northfield Avenue
Edison, NJ 08818
USA

Copyright © 1997 Regency House Publishing Limited

ISBN 0-7858-0837-X

Printed in Italy

Contents

Early Riding Days

Opposite: *An Excelsior motorcycle; the Excelsior company was the third largest U.S. manufacturer behind Harley-Davidson and Indian.*

The first boom in motorcycle manufacture occurred in the years immediately following the turn of the century as the motorcycle made its transition from complex novelty to practical proposition. The automobile was making parallel progress and many of the earliest motorcyclists were adding internal combustion engines to their bicycles. Similarly, the earliest manufacturers of motorcycles were the established bicycle makers who also saw the internal combustion simply as another component to be added on.

The last surviving American motorcycle manufacturer – Harley-Davidson – was founded in 1903 although the number of motorcycles the company made in that first year can be counted on th fingers of one hand. It was not the first either; the Hendee and Hedstrom concern, manufacturers of Indian motorcycles, had been formed in 1901 as a result of the pair's diverse but overlapping interest in the world of competitive bicycling. Because of the vast numbers of motorcycle manufacturers (it would exceed more than 250 different companies eventually), even from the earliest days there was competition to offer the most reliable, fastest, best or cheapest machine. This competition spilled over into race track-type competition as manufacturers began to realize that the spectacle of speed was a draw to crowds eager to see the thrills and spills and to possibly become motorcyclists and therefore customers themselves.

Lubrication systems, starting mechanisms, ignition systems and controls were quickly refined and gradually the accepted formula for motorcycles came to consist of hand throttle, foot clutch, hand gear-change. Final drive was either by leather belt or chain and both were perceived as having advantages and disadvantages although the advent of a functional clutch mechanism ultimately led to chain final drive being favoured for approximately 80 years. Controls were variously mounted on handlebars and in brackets on the sides of gas tanks.

Two engine configurations soon became dominant, namely singles and V-twins, although the U.S. motorcycle industry persevered with in-line air-cooled four-cylinder machines right up until the outbreak of Word War II. As early as 1906 spring forks, purpose-designed frames, and magneto ignition were in use, albeit far from universally. The invention was beginning to catch on and companies had adventurous and exciting names and products: Flying Merkel, Peerless, Cyclone, and advertising copy writers glorified the new form of transport. Iver-Johnson described its motorcycles as 'Exquisite mechanisms', and 'Hit the Indian to trail ... to health and high adventure' said Indian and 'No limit to speed but the law' boasted Reading Standard.

The motorcycle marque known as Indian came into existence as a result of the efforts and collaboration of two men, George Hendee and Oscar Hedstrom, and their combined interest in pedal cycles for, at the turn of the

Opposite: *Lonnie Isam, a Texas motorcycle collector, with his 1905 Harley-Davidson single. On the bench behind him is one from 1907, the oldest unrestored Harley in the world.*

century, bicycle racing was a major sport in both America and Europe. Often, races were held on specially constructed tracks known as velodromes, the technique of slipstreaming being established to enable solo cyclists to attain higher speeds: they would be slipstreamed by a tandem until the arrival of pacing machines powered by internal combustion engines. These machines originated in France and most often used De Dion Bouton engines. Inevitably, certain of these pacing machines were imported into the United States; this happened in 1898 and they were seen at New York's Madison Square Garden Velodrome in 1899. Unfortunately, their reliability was not all it might have been and they often broke down. For the 1900 season, the youthful Oscar Hedstrom constructed an American-made pacing machine. He was an ardent cyclist, both as racer and as proponent of the machine as a means of mass transportation. George Hendee had become involved in cycle manufacture in the Springfield, Massachusetts area and subsequently became involved in cycle race promotion. This endeavour brought him into contact with the man who had constructed the pacing machine and from this would develop the Hendee Manufacturing Company and its Indian Motocycles. The Federation of American Motorcyclists (FAM) was founded late in 1903 and went on to become the American Motorcycle Association (AMA) and the sport of motorcycling's governing body.

In 1909 a construction engineer, Jack Prince, who had built velodromes, began construction of a larger track for use by motorcycles in Los Angeles, California. It was named the Coliseum and two riders came west to race there – Jake De Rosier and Fred Huyck from Chicago and De Rosier, who was to become famous on the boards, set some speed records. Soon there was a board track in Springfield, also built by Prince but partially financed by Hendee to ensure a competition venue

on Indian's home ground. The age of motorcycle racing as a mass spectator sport had arrived. Newspaper coverage was high and racing reportage filled with superlatives. Particularly memorable board-track events include the race between Charles 'Fearless' Balke and Ray Seymour at Elmhurst, California over 50 miles (80km). Balke rode for Excelsior and Seymour for Indian; the race was neck and neck for the entire distance although Seymour took the win by a wheel-length when he attempted overtaking on the last lap.

It was a ruthless, dangerous sport for the participants: Jake De Rosier was unlucky when he raced at Guttenberg in New Jersey where he was in collision with a rider named Frank Hart. De Rosier was not badly injured but Hart broke a leg. At a race at the Los Angeles Motordrome on 10 March 1912 worse luck awaited De Rosier when racing against Fearless Balke, both of them riding Excelsiors. De Rosier employed his usual tactic of slipstreaming a rider until he knew he could pull out and pass. Balke is reported to have been looking over his shoulder as De Rosier made his move when Balke lost control, swerving across De Rosier's path. The motorcycles collided and Jake De Rosier flew into the air and was thrown against the top fence of the track. The famous racer was not killed but severely injured which resulted in two major operations in a Los Angeles hospital before he was well enough to return to Springfield, Massachusetts to convalesce. During this period he campaigned for improvements to the sport, including the introduction of compulsory helmets and goggles for racers, together with higher fences and ways of keeping novices and intoxicated riders off the track. However, he would not live to see such things implemented. Almost a year later, still unwell and in Springfield, he underwent another operation. He died on 25 February 1913 from complications during surgery. His death shocked the

The twenties was the era of the board track racer; this is a 1920 Harley-Davidson built for the short but dangerous board track circuits and originally raced by Dewey Sims.

Thor manufactured board-track racers such as this 1913 V-twin racer although its moment of glory came in 1908 when rider Howard Shafer broke a range of established records ranging from 23–48 miles (37–77km) and established new records for 49–56 miles (79–90km) during a one-hour race at the Los Angeles Agricultural Park dirt track. In 1914 Bill Brier, riding a Thor racer, finished second behind an Indian in the Dodge City 300. This 300-mile (480-km) race was at the time America's most renowned.

American motorcycling world; one newspaper in tribute to him wrote: 'There was but one Jake De Rosier, there will never be another, for the conditions under which he achieved fame will never return.' It was true: his death and the horrific deaths of six spectators and two riders – Ray Seymour and Indian rider Eddie Hasha – at a race in Newark, New Jersey in September 1912 repulsed audiences, and the advent of World War I, the rising cost of timber from which to build tracks, and the oncoming Depression all contributed to the demise of board-track racing.

Accounts of the 1913 Federation of American Motorcyclists (FAM) convention gives an indication of what motorcycling was like in those early days. The holding of the

meeting in Denver was itself a departure as it was the first time such an event had been held west of the Mississippi River. The convention was being hosted by the Colorado Motorcycle Club who had premises at the junction of Colfax Avenue and 14th Street. Motorcyclists began arriving in Denver on 21 July 1913 when a group of 40 riders from Chicago, Milwaukee, and the Dakotas arrived late in the afternoon having covered the 125 miles (200km) from Stirling, Colorado that day; a group numbering 133 arrived the next day from Kansas and the Southern States, accompanied from Colorado Springs by members of the Colorado Motorcycle Club. Among this group was the President of FAM, Dr E. J. Patterson, who had ridden in from his home in Pratt, Kansas,

Right: A 1913 V-twin Pope motorcycle with the then innovative plunger rear suspension. It is owned by Alan Francis of Oxfordshire, England.

and six women riders on their own machines. One of these female riders was E. J.'s daughter, Inez, who at 17 years of age had already made two motorcycle trips from Kansas to New York City accompanied by her father. On 23 July, a Wednesday, another group of riders arrived but, due to the condition of the roads as a result of heavy rain in the Midwest, had come by train with their bikes. Those riders already in Denver rode to the station to meet the train and it is estimated that a total of 400 motorcycles paraded back to the clubhouse. The column of motorcycles was escorted by members of the Denver Police Department and events were, needless to say, heavily reported in the *Denver Post.*

The experience of two stragglers from Kansas who also arrived in Denver on the same day gives some indication of how tough biking could get in America's vast open spaces. Harry Williams was an employee of the Pope company and had ridden his Pope motorcycle from Detroit to Hutchinson, Kansas, where he had met up with the Kansas party and ridden with them to Canon City, Colorado where another rider, Charles Pierce, also on a Pope motorcycle, had broken down. Harry Williams stayed behind to help fix the disabled machine and both riders left for Denver 24 hours behind the main group and, intent on making up for lost time, rode through a severe thunderstorm. The pair crashed when a bolt of lightning struck the road immediately ahead of them. Both bikes, though damaged, could still be ridden and the pair continued until the road became impassable within 10 miles (16km) of Denver. They finally covered the last miles riding between the rails of the Santa Fe railtrack!

Another motorcyclist with experience of riding in adverse conditions was also in Denver for the convention. Billy Teubner had been heralded a hero in the Dayton, Ohio flood of the spring of the same year after riding his motorcycle

Steven Wright's Indian board-track racer dates from 1914 and motorcycles such as this approached speeds of 100mph (160km/h) on tracks made from numerous strips of planking banked on the corners. As many as 20,000 people attended races in the heyday of the sport.

around the outlying areas of Dayton, warning residents of rising waters and giving the alarm as flooding worsened; his actions allowed thousands to escape. He had made Denver from Indianapolis in 14 days. Another rider from Ohio, Jesse Campbell, Ohio commissioner for the FAM, had covered 1,700 miles (2736km) in ten days – a respectable daily average – given the condition of the roads.

The racing division of the convention was scheduled for the weekend beginning that Friday and noted racers began to

arrive in Denver to take part. Indian riders with factory support, Fearless Balke and Ray Seymour, were there to uphold the honour of the Springfield marque while Red Armstrong arrived, flying the colours of Excelsior. A local rider was among the favourites, M. K. Fredericks – Curly to his friends and fans. Controversy was to arise, however, as two tracks then existed in Denver, the mile-long dirt oval in Overland Park and the massive three-mile board track at Tuileries Park, and it was because of this that the dispute

Motorcycles such as this Miller are real rarities and restoration work has to be extremely painstaking in order to refinish a machine to this standard. Missing, worn, or damaged components have to be made from scratch, simply because spare parts no longer exist.

arose. The popularity of board-track racing was waning because of the perceived dangers to both riders and spectators; the board-track proprietors wanted the racing run on their track while the FAM insisted it was run on dirt and it looked as though that was the way the championship would be decided. This was not the end of the matter, however, as two people well known within the fledgeling world of motorcycling were at odds with one another over the very issue of board-track racing.

Dr. J. P. Thornley of New York, Chairman of the National Competitions Committee was accused of siding with board-track race promoters by T. J. Sullivan, editor of a motorcycling magazine. Violence was avoided, though only by firm control from the chair by President Patterson. Later in the evening the two individuals accidentally met in the nearby Albany Hotel where a fight ensued and other delegates had to separate them. The various committees attempted to resolve some of the problems in an attempt to restore a modicum of decorum

Opposite: *An Excelsior owner riding his four-cylinder machine at an Antique Motorcycle Club of America spring event at Eustis, Florida, in 1997. The association was founded during the fifties and has members worldwide as well as a busy annual calendar.*

to the proceedings, even though the question of where to hold the races was still not fully resolved. However, a compromise was reached. The official races would be held on Friday, Saturday and Sunday morning on dirt and an unofficial race would be held on Sunday afternoon on the board track. This decided, the evening's dance at the Colorado Motorcycle Club was generally acknowledged to have been a great success. The next day saw elections for FAM committee posts which were seen by many as contests between East and West Coasts although Patterson retained his position as President. Now that the business of the convention was resolved, the delegates went riding in the foothills of the Rockies west of the city taking in such places as Morrison, Golden, Lookout Mountain and Clear Creek Canyon.

Racing was divided between amateur and professional events; scheduled for Friday were amateur and professional races for stock motorcycles. A Brooklyn rider – John Constant – won the 1-, 2-, 5- and 25-mile races on a V-twin Indian, averaging in excess of 60mph (100km/h) in each race. His time for the 25 miles (40km) was 24.14 minutes. During the 5-mile (8-km) race the handlebars of his machine broke and he was forced to complete the event riding one-handed. Fearless Balke won the 5- and 10-mile professional races at a somewhat faster pace. The 10 miles (16 km) took 8.47 minutes.

Saturday's races got off to a delayed start due to rain but had the effect of dampening down the dust. The Manufacturer's Association Five Mile Cup race was won by Will Feuerstein from Norfolk, Virginia in 5.11 minutes. The professional 1-miler of the day saw a new record set by Fearless Balke of 51 seconds dead. Later the 10-mile professional race developed into a game of dice between Balke and Robert Perry from Chicago. In the last lap Balke's Indian began to misfire and Perry took the flag. Red Armstrong was

placed third. The Sunday morning programme included 5- and 10-mile professional races, both of which were again won by Robert Perry who set a new record for 10 miles (16 km) at 8.28 minutes. Soon after the successful convention drew to a close, FAM became the Motorcycle and Allied Trades Association (MATA) and later still the American Motorcycle Association (AMA).

The popularity of motorcycle racing took a downward turn in the early twenties, the deaths of a number of racers being partially to blame. Bob Perry, who rode for Excelsior, was killed in an accident while testing an overhead camshaft racer for the company at the Ascot Speedway in Los Angeles on 4 January 1920 and Ignatz Schwinn cancelled all his company's racing activities immediately afterwards. Indian and Harley-Davidson were still involved, however, and set out to contest the 300-mile (480-km) National in Dodge City, Kansas on 4 July 1921. Indian had seven riders mounted on Franklin's Powerplus-derived sidevalves known as pocket-valves. Harley-Davidson entered Ralph Hepburn on an eight-valve machine and five other riders on twin-cam pocket-valve Harleys. A privateer, Waldo Korn, entered the race on an Excelsior. The victory, in what was the last-ever Kansas 300-miler, went to Hepburn and Harley-Davidson. Soon afterwards, Harley-Davidson too would retire temporarily from racing.

The board track phenomenon had not entirely passed and races were still being promoted. There were enough reckless 'devil may care' riders willing to risk all out on the boards and crowds more than eager to watch their exploits and sample the other attractions of the events; it was reported that prostitutes openly solicited, illegal betting was conducted and bootleg liquor openly sold. It is hardly surprising that the transitory nature of the racers' lives and the excitement that

Opposite: When Bill Henderson left Henderson and set up the Ace company in 1919 to manufacture in-line four-cylinder motorcycles, he redesigned the inlet and exhaust valve configuration of the engine for his models from 1920 onwards. In 1922 'Cannonball' Baker, a rider famous for record-setting rides on Indians, set a transcontinental record aboard an Ace Four but later in the same year Henderson was killed in a motorcycle accident which led ultimately to the demise of the company. Eventually it was acquired by Indian, in 1927, who for a couple of years manufactured the fours as Indian Aces before simply calling them Indian Fours.

the events generated encouraged uproarious behaviour. One group of racers who arrived in Chicago to take part in events at the Riverview Park Motordrome are reported to have pooled their resources and rented an entire brothel for the three days prior to the race! However, many felt that the many dangers and correspondingly high accident rates caused motorcycling to be perceived in a negative light which may have contributed to a decline in sales, especially when the press began to refer to Motordrome as 'Murderdrome'.

While Indian was still interested in promoting its motorcycles through racing, the effect of such promotion was weakened as neither the Harley-Davidson nor the Excelsior factories were engaged in racing at the time. Indian subsequently reduced its racing budget and competition motorcycling of this type consequently suffered a decline. Charles Gustafson Jr. supervised racing efforts during this period andAlbert 'Shrimp' Burns, Charles 'Fearless' Balke and Paul Bower, the latter too young to have earned a nickname, were all killed in separate racing accidents. Hillclimb competition increased in popularity and Indian riders achieved some endurance records. 'Cannonball' Baker rode an Indian Scout from New York City to Los Angeles, California in 179 hours 28 minutes. Over the 3,368 miles (5,420km) of the journey he used 40 gallons (182 litres) of gasoline and 5 gallons (23 litres) of lubricating oil. He averaged 20mph (32km/h). The 300-mile (490-km) National was held in Wichita, Kansas, in 1923, and was won by Curly Fredericks on a 61-cubic inch Indian.

Despite the general prosperity enjoyed by the United States in 1924, the year saw an ever-declining domestic market for motorcycles, Henderson Fours being produced in smaller numbers, Ace in serious difficulties financially and Excelsior having to cut back on its production. The reason for this was

nothing to do with bad publicity concerning racing or immoral behaviour at racetracks but simply the new availability of the cheap mass-produced car. A Model T Ford was by now cheaper than a sidecar outfit. Sales to law enforcement agencies continued to be important to Indian and other motorcycle manufacturers but these sales were not enough on their own. The Great Depression, heralded by the Wall Street Crash of 1929, saw the end of most of the remaining U.S. manufacturers and another, Excelsior, was not able to withstand the pressure and closed in 1931 leaving Indian as Harley-Davidson's only domestic competitor. Even these larger companies were lucky to survive this dark period of America's economic history.

The Manufacturers

ACE

This company was founded by William Henderson in Philadelphia in 1919 after he had sold his previous company, Henderson (see below), to Ignatz Schwinn. The Ace company also produced in-line four-cylinder motorcycles to his design. The first machines had a capacity of 1168cc and this was subsequently increased. Henderson was killed in a motorcycle accident while testing a new machine in 1922 and the company continued in business with Arthur Lemon as designer. Ace engines were of the inlet-over-exhaust design and fitted with alloy pistons. The company experienced financial difficulties and was acquired by Indian in 1927. The new owners transferred production to Springfield, Massachusetts and named the machines Indian Ace. After 1929 the models were simply called Indian Fours.

CLEVELAND

Cleveland was one of a plethora of short-lived American motorcycle manufacturers. It was in business between 1915 and 1929 and in 1922 took over Reading Standard. The motorcycles built by Cleveland are acknowledged to have been of sound design and started off with a 269cc two-stroke. In 1924 it produced a 347cc single-cylinder-engined motorcycle with an inlet-over-exhaust engine followed by a

746cc in-line four. This latter machine was refined in 1928 and the capacity increased to 996cc but was unable to compete with the Henderson and Ace Fours. The Wall Street Crash of 1929 forced the company out of business despite the quality of its products.

Right and opposite: Among the ideas tried out by Al Crocker was an overhead-valve conversion for Indian's 101 Scout. This 101 Scout has been equipped with a replica of Crocker's ohv conversion manufactured by Gwen Banquer of Port St. Lucie, Florida. The extra components on top of the cylinder heads are clearly visible in both photographs. It is unusual to se the Crocker logo on the gas tank and the Indian name cast into the primary case.

CROCKER

Albert Crocker was a Los Angeles Indian dealer, involved in the motorcycle business, who began to make and sell his own brand of motorcycles. He graduated from university in Illinois and went to work for the Aurora Automatic Machine Company who made Thor motorcycles. Riding one of its machines he won numerous events, including endurance runs. Later he joined the Hendee Manufacturing Company, maker of Indian motorcycles and made friends with both Hendee and Hedstrom, President and Chief Engineer respectively. He later moved to Colorado and managed the Denver Indian office. While there, Al Crocker married Gertrude Jefford, the widow of racer Eddie Hasha who had been killed in a tragic accident at the Newark, New Jersey board track. From Denver, Crocker was sent to run the Indian dealership in San Francisco where he met Hap Alzina. He moved south to Los Angeles in the twenties and became the SoCal Indian distributor with premises on Venice Boulevard. He rode the bikes he sold and, with the introduction of the 101 Scout, sales boomed. Crocker was a capable designer and engineer and relinquished his Indian dealership to go into the manufacturing side of the business. He started with speedway competition bikes of which he made 31. Crocker produced his own engines, including an overhead camshaft chain-drive machine for speedway. The machines enjoyed success on the tracks until JAP upgraded its engines to reduce competition from the Crocker units. Al Crocker began production of his eponymous 61 cu in V-twin motorcycles in 1936 which was coincidentally the year that Harley-Davidson introduced its first overhead valve 61 cu in machine. Crocker's engine was a 45° V-twin with hemi-spherical combustion chambers and dome-top pistons. The cylinders were sufficiently thick to allow overbores of up to 90 cu in and finned for cooling. The first bikes had exposed pushrods and rockers but the later 75 cu in V-twins featured enclosed assemblies. The valves were positioned side by side in the cylinder top and dual oil pumps were standard equipment. The transmission case was cast into the heavy-gauge tubular frame and featured heavy duty gears to eliminate any chance of failure. The clutch was of a wet design similar to that used by Indian.

Crockers have been described as the Duesenburgs of American motorcycles and were fast bikes. They are reputed to have been capable of cruising at between 90 and 100mph (160km/h) with a top speed in excess of 110mph (177km/h), speeds which were little short of phenomenal in 1936. Most Crockers were fitted with sprung solo saddles and elements of the styling of Crocker motorcycles later found their way into bobbers and subsequently choppers, including short rear fenders and scalloped paint schemes.

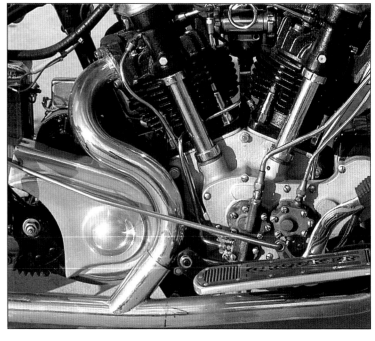

Above: *Albert Crocker manufactured a small number of single-cylinder overhead-valve speedway bikes for competition use. They were intended to compete with the British-manufactured JAP-engined speedway racers of the day and initially had some success. The machines to which Crocker gave his name and for which he is justifiably famous are, however, the sporting roadgoing V-twins he built in the years prior to World War II. They were fast machines built to a high standard. Details included the maker's name cast into the* steering damper handle (above right), the enclosed pushrod assemblies of the later models (below right) and a number of contemporary custom-style touches, including scalloped paint schemes and bobbed fenders (opposite). The handle for the tank-mounted gear shifter of this bike was in the form of a dice – a custom touch from the thirties and forties.*

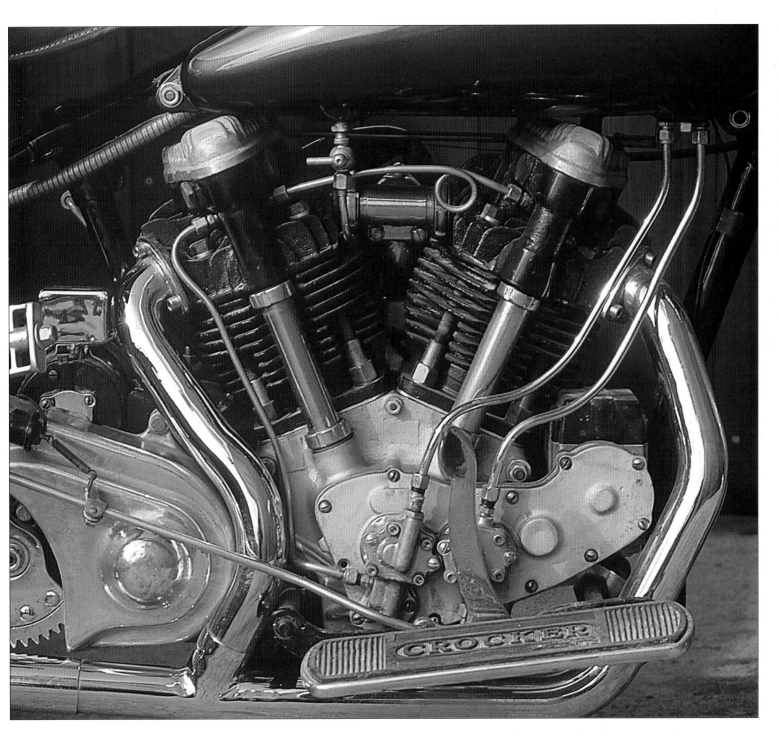

Left and opposite: *This Crocker is owned by Dave Hansen of The Shop, Ventura, California. It is one of the later machines featuring as it does the enclosed pushrods for the overhead valve assembly. The valves were positioned side by side in the cylinder heads. The dual oil pumps seen on the engine were standard Crocker engineering. It has been suggested that Crocker lost money on every one of these V-twin motorcycles he made and sold. Production ceased at the outbreak of World War II.*

Many aspects of Crocker motorcycle design were reminiscent of Indian and Harley-Davidson motorcycles, simply because that was the styling in vogue at the time. The tank-mounted dash (above) features a Corbin speedo as well as a C for Crocker cast into the dash cover. The girder forks (right) are similar to those used by Indian but Crocker was careful to avoid infringing the patents of other manufacturers.

CYCLONE

The Cyclone was produced for only four years by the Joerns Motor Manufacturing Company from 1239 Hampden Avenue, St. Paul, Minnesota but was in that short period highly acclaimed. The V-twin, introduced in 1913 had overhead camshafts and displaced 996cc. It was the most technologically advanced motorcycle of its day featuring as it did a roller bearing mounted crankshaft and connecting rods, a bevel-driven camshaft and forged steel flywheels of a spoked design. The machining was so accurate that shims were not required to meet maximum end float of .001 inches for the camshaft drive. The performance of a Cyclone was notably fast for the times and the famous yellow Cyclone racers took so many race victories that they became almost legendary, especially after the company went out of business following the 1916 race season.

The distinctive yellow Cyclones were built by Joerns Motor Manufacturing of St. Paul, Minnesota between 1913 and 1915. For a brief period they were highly renowned both on and off the race tracks of America.

Opposite left: *Cyclone used rigid frames for its race bikes and quarter elliptic leaf springs for its roadgoing models, this being a roadgoing model as it has the rear suspension assembly. The quarter elliptic spring can be seen positioned vertically behind the seat post to allow the triangular rear portion of the frame to move as the machine crosses uneven surfaces.*

Opposite right: *The Cyclone's engine, designed by Andrew Strands, was advanced for its time. It features overhead camshafts which rotated in opposite directions; the cam towers were made in two parts and, although they are reputed to have had a tendency to stretch and flex at high revs, the Cyclones were capable of speeds approaching 100mph (160km/h).*

Left: *The racing Cyclones had rigid front forks but the roadgoing models had trailing link forks, the racing and roadgoing Cyclones otherwise differing only in small details. A rider named Don Johns won the Sacramento, California One Mile National Championship on a Cyclone racer in July 1915.*

The outstanding feature of the Cyclone engine
was the overhead camshaft valve arrangement.
Through bevel-geared shafts that ran in tubes
up the sides of the cylinders, the required
timing for valve opening was achieved. The
front cylinder shaft also drove the magneto
drive shaft via a bevel gear. The complex
arrangement of two-piece shafts to allow
cylinder removal and bearings worked well.

EMBLEM

Emblem motorcycles were assembled in Angola, New York by the Emblem Manufacturing Company between 1907 and 1925. Like many other brands, the first models utilized Aurora-Thor castings for the engine which was mounted in place of much of the seat post in a diamond-type bicycle frame. By 1909 the company was making its own engines which were installed in a loop frame and were belt-driven. Production of a V-twin-engined bike started in 1910 and by 1913 it displaced 76.6 cu in (1254 cc). The company exported much of its later output to Europe. The 1910 single featured a combined gas and oil tank that fitted around the top tube of the frame, a solo saddle and flat steel fenders. It featured spring forks and a contracting band rear brake as well as final drive by means of a leather belt. The carburettor was a proprietary item from the Heitger Carburettor Company of 1111 Beecher Street, Indianapolis, Indiana and the optional magneto was made by Ruthardt. Other companies using Heitger carburettors included Merkel, Yale, Marvel, Waverley, American of Chicago, Greyhound, Armac and New Era.

Emblem motorcycles were manufactured by the Emblem Manufacturing Company of Angola, New York between 1907 and 1925. Its V-twins were offered in 1911 with either flat or Vee belt drive while an engine equipped with a clutch and known as the 'free' engine was available as an option. By 1913 Emblem had the distinction of being the producers of the largest capacity V-twin of the time, a 76.6 cu in (1255cc) unit. The single hexagonal nut seen in the centre of the timing case cover indicates that this is a 1913 or later Emblem V-twin.

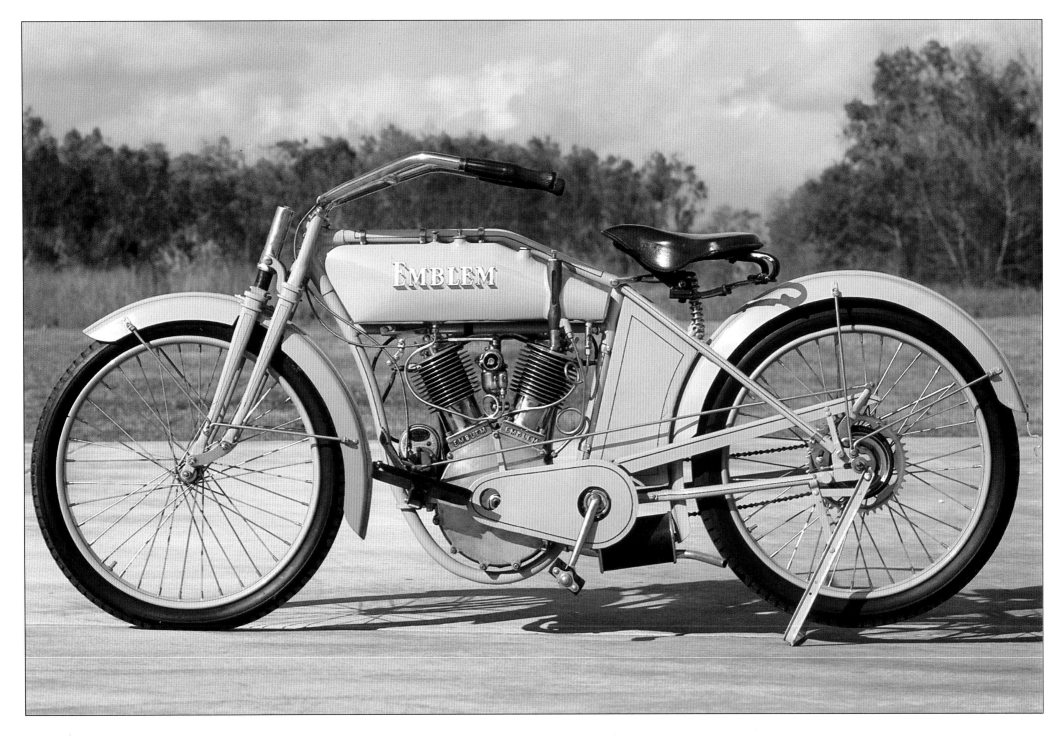

1913 Emblem V-twin (specification)

Country of Origin	*U.S.A.*
Capacity	*1255cc (76.6 cu in)*
Engine Cycle	*Four stroke*
Number of Cylinders	*Two*
Top Speed	*40mph (64km/h)*
Power	*4 hp*
Transmission	*Three speed*
Frame	*Tubular steel*

The Emblem of 1913 (opposite) featured chain primary and final drive and housed a clutch assembly within the primary cover. A loop frame curved around the V-twin engine. The Emblem brand name was cast into the bases of the cylinder barrels (below) and the footboards (left). Ignition was by means of the magneto mounted forward of the front cylinder. The forks (below left) were sprung while the frame was rigid, although U.S. manufacturers were beginning to experiment with rear suspension at the time.

This page and opposite: *An Emblem board-track racer owned by Jim Lattin. The engine features total loss lubrication, a Heitger carburettor, and a belt drive system that is engaged by moving the lever on the side of the tank. The belt is made from leather. The wheels are 26 inches (66cm) in diameter and such machines were regularly raced on board tracks and dirt tracks around the United States. The dangers of the early days of dirt-track racing were epitomized in the accident involving Lee Taylor, a former Emblem racer, who had gone on to ride Indians. At the Hamilton, Ohio, 4th of July dirt-track meeting of 1916, Taylor on an Indian crashed in the dust and was run over by a following racer, Maldwyn Jones. His leg was badly cut and required amputation as a result of gangrene. Sadly, and despite the removal of his leg, he died a week later.*

Below: *Excelsior made its first V-twin, a 61 cu in (1000cc) motorcycle, in 1911 and gradually upgraded it over the next ten years. The first machines were single-speed but by 1914 a two-speed transmission was available and by 1915 a three-speed. This 1919 engine was a continuation of the development, the next major step being the advent of the 74 cu in (1200cc) machine of 1921.*

Opposite: *The Excelsiors of 1917 to 1919 featured valanced fenders and were all finished in olive drab. This one is owned by Dave Hansen of The Shop, Ventura, California.*

EXCELSIOR

Excelsior diversified into motorcycle production in Chicago in 1907. It had already been in business as the Excelsior Supply Company and was to become the Excelsior Motor Manufacturing and Supply Company, having its offices and factory at 22nd and Union Streets, Chicago. Its first machine was a 3.25 hp single that displaced 438.1cc (26.74 cu in) and was typical of the early days of internal combustion engine manufacture. The engine was mounted vertically in a frame clearly derived from a pedal bicycle-type and had a mechanically-operated exhaust valve and an atmospheric inlet valve. This latter valve was opened by the vacuum created in the cylinder bore by the descending piston on the induction stroke. Both valves were mounted in a chamber alongside the cylinder but siamesed into it and this became known as a 'pocket valve'.

Later, the company produced larger capacity single-cylinder machines which also used a pocket-valve design. Following the trend towards V-twins in American motorcycling Excelsior would later drop production of singles after it had been taken over by Ignatz Schwinn, an established bicycle manufacturer in 1911.

The 1912 Excelsior models were competitively priced, the twin with magneto ignition being $250, while the single, available in either battery or magneto configurations, was $200 and $225 respectively. The 1912 twin was finished in a two-colour paint scheme, featured both belt drive and pedals and was based around a V-twin engine in a diamond frame.

By 1913 Excelsior was able to claim to be the manufacturer of the first machines to exceed 100mph (160km/h). In the same year the singles were listed at $200 and produced 4–5 hp while the 7–10 hp V-twins were listed at

$250. The single-cylinder bikes featured a right-hand throttle and left-hand clutch. The company advertised its 'Kumfort Kushion' sprung seat and its rod-operated clutch as two major selling points. Despite the trend towards foot clutches at this time, Excelsior twins featured a right-hand twistgrip throttle and a left-hand clutch. At a series of seven races in Portland, Oregon the same year, Excelsior machines claimed six first places and one second, notable being a single-cylinder machine that covered 5 miles (8km) in five minutes to win its class. A new lightweight machine was listed for 1916 and retailed at $135.

By 1917 the company was based at 3701 Cortland Street, Chicago and, flushed with the success of its machines in the Capistrano and Bakersfield hillclimbs, was advertising its Series 18 models, presumably with an eye to the coming sales year. The Excelsior Series 18 lightweight retailed at $135 and featured a two-stroke single-cylinder engine, a kick starter, two-speed transmission, brakes, footboards and a cushioned seat. The Big Twin X was available for $275 or $310 with electric lights.

Under Schwinn's management, the company had considerable racing success in both board- and dirt-track events. It abruptly withdrew from racing in 1920 after the death of its star rider Bob Perry in an accident at the Los Angeles Speedway while testing a new racer. Ignatz Schwinn is reputed to have smashed the castings of the race bikes with a sledgehammer immediately afterwards. Excelsior ceased manufacturing motorcycles in 1931 after the introduction in 1925 of a 45-cu in V-twin that would become a standard and popular capacity in American motorcycling. This 45 cu in machine was known as the Super-X.

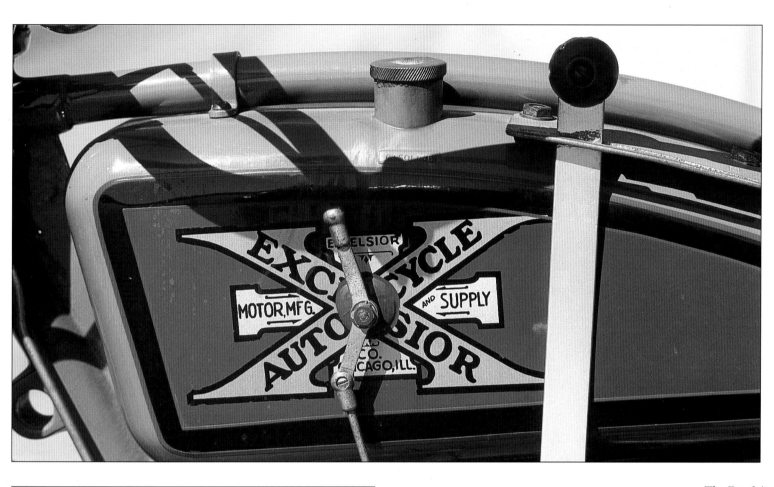 

1919 Excelsior V-twin (specification)	
Country of Origin	U.S.A.
Capacity	992cc (60.5 cu in)
Engine Cycle	Four stroke
Number of Cylinders	Two
Top Speed	95mph (153km/h)
Power	n/a
Transmission	Three speed
Frame	Tubular steel

The Excelsior V-twin engine (opposite) featured valves in the F-head arrangement. Lubrication of the front cylinder was by means of the pipe to its base: this was considered necessary because the front cylinder was not sufficiently lubricated by the oil thrown from the crankshaft and con rod assemblies as was the rear one. The Excelsior featured a foot-clutch/hand-change arrangement for the three-speed transmission; lowest gear was forwards, neutral, second and third were selected by pulling the lever backwards (above right). The magneto ignition timing was controlled by the small lever mounted on the side of the tank in the centre of the Excelsior Autocycle logo (above left).

The Super-X 45 cu in (750cc) appeared in the mid-twenties, had a unit-construction engine and gearbox (far left) and featured helical gears for the primary drive as did Indians of the time. The motorcycle (opposite) was built in 1928 for racing. The first 45-cu in class National Championship race was run in 1926 (won by Indian) and Joe Petrali brought Excelsior/Henderson their first win since 1915 in 1927 in the 10-mile (16-km) 45-cu in race in Milwaukee on a bike such as this one with springer forks (above) and no brakes (left).

The 1914 Flanders 4 (right) was a belt-drive 4 hp single-cylinder motorcycle with a bore and stroke of 3.25 x 3.6 inches and a displacement of 29.41 cubic inches (483cc). The Flanders machines utilized a double-acting spring fork assembly and a diamond frame. These two examples of what are now rare motorcycles are owned by Flanders, the noted aftermarket Harley handlebar and parts manufacturer.

FLANDERS

This was, like so many of the early marques, a short-lived operation, being in production for only three years between 1911 and 1914. The motorcycles were made by the company who also made the Flanders car and its first machine was a 4 hp single with a loop frame. The company introduced a V-twin in 1914 but ceased production in the same year, so few were sold.

Below: *A 1913 Flying Merkel in Lonnie Isam's collection. It is the type of machine also ridden by Maldwyn Jones. The machine featured a mono-shock rear suspension arrangement. The Flying Merkel name (below right) was adopted as a brand name after 1911 (although it was used earlier) when the Miami Cycle Company purchased Merkel Light. The 1910 racer (opposite) was restored by Rick Peterson for Jim Lattin's museum in California. It is a V-twin although a single-cylinder version of the racer was also offered.*

FLYING MERKEL

In 1902 Joseph Merkel began to manufacture motorcycles in Layton Park, Milwaukee, Wisconsin with his own design of single-cylinder engine with atmospheric inlet valves, going on to produce a V-twin. He also designed a spring frame and was the first U.S. manufacturer to market it. These bikes were sold as Merkel motorcycles but in 1909 Merkel merged with the Light Manufacturing and Foundry Company of Pottstown, Pennsylvania who made Thor-engined machines and the company became known as the Merkel Light Motor Company.

From 1910 the motorcycles were referred to as Flying Merkels. The company was acquired by the Miami Cycle Company in 1911 and transferred production to its base in Middletown, Ohio. The Miami Cycle Company produced the Racycle, also using Aurora-Thor engine castings mounted in the seat post of a bicycle-type diamond frame. They dropped the Racycle name when, apart from using it on a lightweight machine, they acquired Merkel. Joe Merkel left the company in 1913. In 1916 it was possible to buy a Miami Power Bicycle for $115: it was a lightweight single-cylinder-engined machine in a diamond frame. Production ended in 1917.

Lonnie Isam's 1905 Harley-Davidson single-cylinder motorcycle (right and opposite). This machine dates from Harley's third year of production and features a loop frame designed especially for the motorcycle rather than a diamond bicycle-type frame. The oil and gas tanks were attached to the frame by leather straps, the gas tank being the larger of the two, and the oil tank was mounted to the rear of the engine cylinder. The leather straps endured until 1908. The single-cylinder engine was the inlet-over-exhaust F-head configuration and displacement was less than 30 cubic inches (492cc).

HARLEY-DAVIDSON

The now legendary Harley-Davidson company was founded early in the century in Milwaukee, Wisconsin by William S. Harley and Arthur Davidson and the other Davidson brothers, William and Walter, later joined the firm, too. Bill Harley and Arthur Davidson worked evenings and weekends to produce their earliest machines in a shed in the Davidsons' backyard – their first factory. In 1903 they built a single-cylinder motorcycle that displaced approximately 10 cu in (160cc). It worked well but lacked hill-climbing ability which led to the building of two improved motorcycles in 1904 which they intended to sell, the Davidson brothers' Aunt Janet pinstriping the finished machines prior to their sale. From then on the company was in business and production grew exponentially: in 1905 the group made eight motorcycles, 50 in 1906, 150 in 1907 and over 400 in 1908. Their 1905 motorcycles were singles of 25 cu in (405cc) displacement in a bicycle-style frame with belt drive and no brakes so that the rider had to pedal backwards in order to slow down.

The Silent Gray Fellow was the first model produced in significant numbers by the workforce that now numbered six. It was still a single and so named because of its quiet running and standard grey paint scheme.

The company filed its incorporation papers in 1907, the two families retaining a controlling portion of the stock right up until the company was sold to the American Machine and Foundry Company (AMF) in 1969.

Harley-Davidson's first V-twin was introduced in 1909 but its first really successful one was marketed in 1911. A chain drive version appeared in 1912 and in 1913 Harley-Davidson sold 12,904 motorcycles and export sales began.

During World War I, Harley-Davidson supplied half its

output to the U.S. Army and began to prepare for post-war production, which included expanding the factory. The company suffered a drop in sales in the early twenties as a result of competition from low-priced automobiles but managed to retain a strong export market.

The oil tank on the 1905 Harley-Davidson single (left) fits under the gas tank but extends up into it to give sufficient capacity for the oil. Engine oiling is by total loss. Drive for the first Harleys was by means of a belt that was engaged and tensioned by a lever arrangement (above). The 1907 Harley seen (opposite) on Lonnie Isam's work bench is truly a piece of history as it is believed to be the world's oldest original and unrestored Harley-Davidson motorcycle.

In the years immediately following the Armistice, exports to Europe were resumed and in 1921 Douglas Davidson (no relation), aboard a Harley-Davidson, became the first person to exceed 100mph on a motorcycle in Britain, recording a speed of 100.76mph (162km/h) at the famous English racing circuit, Brooklands. The year was not altogether an auspicious one for the company because sales were down more than 18,000 on 1920's record high of 28,189 and for the first time the company made a loss, one of the reasons for the slump in sales being Ford's mass-produced car, the Model T, which was selling for almost the same price as a sidecar outfit when approximately 75 per cent of Harley Davidson's machines were leaving the factory equipped with sidecars.

Exports did not suffer as badly and the Harley-Davidson company embarked on a programme to boost sales around the globe. An employee, Alfred Rich Child, visited Cape Town in South Africa and rode north the full length of the African continent on a J Model. En route he sold 400 motorcycles and established a number of new dealers.

The Wall Street Crash and its effects devastated Harley-Davidson's sales until they bottomed out in 1933 with sales of only 3,703 bikes. In 1936 it introduced the EL Knucklehead, its

Opposite: *This Harley-Davidson racer dates from 1916 and is powered by an inlet-over-exhaust V-twin. Machines such as this were built for the dangerous environment of the board and dirt tracks and a meeting typical of the times was held on 22 June 1919 at Ascot Park in California. It was a 200-mile (320-km) event on dirt and 10,000 spectators turned up to watch. Two Harley riders, Ralph Hepburn and Ray Weishar vied for the lead of the first portion of the race. They both had to stop for fuel and tyres and Hepburn got away first and held this place until the end. He had achieved a record speed of 72.32mph (116km/h). Harley-Davidsons took the first five places, relegating the competing Indians and Excelsiors to sixth place and below.*

first overhead valve-engined motorcycle which was an instant success. Unionization of the workforce occurred in 1937 and the first of the founders died in the same year. The others would pass away in 1942, 1943 and 1950. World War II interrupted civilian motorcycle production and Harley-Davidson manufactured in excess of 88,000 sidevalve 45cu in motorcycles for the various allied armies. These bikes later popularized Harley-Davidsons around the world, particularly in parts of Europe.

The Milwaukee factory had developed the overhead-valve design of engine parallel to its refinements of the sidevalve engine. It was designated the 61E Model, the 61 equating to its displacement in cubic inches (1000cc). The engine was soon referred to as the 'Knucklehead' because of the way its rocker covers were said to resemble knuckles. The Knucklehead was the first Harley to have dry sump lubrication (oil recirculating between oil tank and engine) instead of a total loss system. The oil tank – horseshoe-shaped – was located under the seat, the engine was fitted into a double loop frame and a new style of gas tank appeared. It was made in two halves, hid the frame tubes, and had the speedo set into a dash plate that fitted between the two halves of the tank.

Once post-war production was back to normal, the Panhead engine appeared and Harley enjoyed boom years despite competition from huge numbers of imported British motorcycles. By the mid-sixties its U.S. market share had contracted considerably and as little as 3 per cent of production was exported. The future was uncertain and in 1968 the American Machine and Foundry Company (AMF), a huge conglomerate, was one of two companies showing interest in a takeover. They took control in January 1969.

The years that followed were something of a mixed

blessing for Harley-Davidson; productivity increased but quality control decreased to the extent that AMF bikes failed to gain a good reputation. The company were also obliged to face another wave of imports directed at its U.S. market, this time from Japan. Despite a number of new products, by 1980 AMF was looking at ways of disposing of Harley-Davidson and accepted a management buyout by 13 of Harley-Davidson's executives. The biggest news, besides the change of ownership, was the first all-new Big Twin engine since 1965 – the Evolution engine – for which much of the development work had been under AMF. The Evolution engine put Harley-Davidson back on the road to success and undoubtedly made it the strong company it is today and the last surviving American motorcycle manufacturer.

During its history, the company has experimented with a number of smaller capacity motorcycles, including an opposed twin. This twin-cylinder engine was of a type more common to British manufacturers, such as Douglas.

The Boxer twin was arranged longitudinally in the frame rather than across it like the much later experimental XA motorcycle for the U.S. Army. It was a small capacity machine with a 37 cu-in displacement (606cc) engine and was produced in limited numbers in 1920. It featured an external flywheel but its overall style resembled the V-twin Harleys of the time.

The Hummer was a post-war lightweight from Harley-Davidson – an 125cc DKW-inspired machine in the post-war years; then came the Aermacchi lightweights in the sixties and the successful Sportsters which has been part of its range since the K Model of 1952.

The factory-designed racers featured engine plates rather than tubular lower frames and engine mounts. By this time chain final drive was standard on motorcycles. Harley-Davidson had considerable racing success and eventually withdrew from race involvement as it felt it had little effect on sales. Walter Davidson pointed out that even after their motorcycles had been ridden to wins in three consecutive Dodge City 300-milers, the Police Department of that city continued to ride Indian motorcycles!

1906 Silent Gray Fellow

The Silent Gray Fellow was so named because of its quiet running, as a result of its muffler, and its Renault grey paint scheme. The engine size of the model was sequentially increased from 405cc (25 cu in) when introduced to 500cc (30 cu in) in 1909 and 565cc (35 cu in) in 1913. Other changes made in the duration of the production run were to the design of the cylinder head cooling fins and a reshaping of the front downtube of the frame. The gas tank was redesigned in 1912 and 1916 while belt drive was discontinued in 1914. Production of all singles ended in 1918 with the trend towards V-twins by American manufacturers. V-twins were seen as a way to increase the power of a motorcycle engine cheaply and the design fitted existing frames.

1906 Silent Gray Fellow (specification)	
Country of Origin	U.S.A.
Capacity	405cc (25 cu in)
Engine Cycle	Four stroke
Number of Cylinders	One
Top Speed	50mph (80km/h)
Power	n/a
Transmission	Single speed
Frame	Steel Loop

1915 Model 11-E

This machine was a Harley-Davidson V-twin-engined motorcycle that developed 11 hp, hence its designation. The motorcycle was based around a double bar loop frame and was fitted with sprung forks of Harley-Davidson design. The overall diameter of the wheels was 28 inches (70cm) and each wheel had 40 spokes. The 11-E had an angular tank that contained a total of 15 pints (8.5 litres). The oil tank was of 5 pints (3 litres) capacity. A solo saddle and luggage rack were fitted to the machine as were a pair of fenders, the rear one being curved while the front was flat with valanced sides. The whole machine was finished in Harley-Davidson grey and nickel plate.

1915 Model 11-E (specification)

Country of Origin	*U.S.A.*
Capacity	*1000cc (61 cu in)*
Engine Cycle	*Four stroke*
Number of Cylinders	*Two*
Top Speed	*50mph (80km/h)*
Power	*11 hp*
Transmission	*Single speed*
Frame	*Steel Loop*

A 1913 Harley-Davidson V-twin (opposite) owned by Dave Hansen. The grey V-twin features the sloping top tube to make saddle fitment (left), introduced in 1912, easier and the straight downtube was introduced in 1911 along with its first practical V-twin engine (above left). Also from 1911 were the vertical fins on the cylinder heads. The clutch (far left) accommodated the two-speed transmission that would become a three-speed in 1915. The forks were sprung although the springs were enclosed (above right) and brakes and electric lights were yet to come.

The Federation of American Motorcyclists (FAM) folded during 1919 and in its place came MATA – the Motorcycle and Allied Trades Association – under whose auspices the 200-mile (320-km) Marion, Indiana race was run on 1 September. Forty laps were required to cover the 200 miles. The Harley team riders included Ray Weishar, Ralph Hepburn, Leslie Parkhurst, Maldwyn Jones, Otto Walker and Shrimp Burns. Harley won, although Indian's Teddy Carroll posed a serious challenge for the lead until an exhaust valve spring failed on his machine during the 39th lap. Despite this, he finished fourth behind Parkhurst, Hepburn and Walker respectively. This racer (right) is typical of those days, with its drop handlebars (opposite left) long gas tank and oil pump (opposite top right). The engines (opposite bottom right) were built in both single and twin cam configurations, the twin cammers being faster, and were supplied to factory racers and others favoured by the company.

1930 VL Model

The V Model series was an almost entirely new motorcycle when it was introduced, sharing few parts with its F-head predecessor. Around 13 variants of the sidevalve V Models were produced through the production run that had variations in specifications such as those equipped with magnetos and higher compression bikes. The V Series became the U Series in 1937 with the introduction of dry sump lubrication.

1930 VL Model (specification)	
Country of Origin	U.S.A.
Capacity	1207cc (73.66 cu in)
Engine Cycle	Four stroke
Number of Cylinders	Two
Top Speed	85mph (137km/h)
Power	n/a
Transmission	Three speed
Frame	Steel loop

Later versions of Harley's F-head racers, such as the one opposite, had lower frames which necessitated cut-outs in the side of the gas tank (left) in order to clear the valve rockers. This is a single cam machine as revealed by the shape of the cam-case cover (bottom right). The oil pump for the total loss lubrication system is located on the side of the tank where it could be operated at speed by the rider's left hand (bottom left). In October 1919 the Harley team raced at the two-mile board track in Sheepshead Bay, New York. Weishar was on an eight-valve Harley and broke the record for 50 miles (80km) that had been set in 1913 by Lee Humiston. Shrimp Burns and Maldwyn Jones took the 1st and 2nd places for Harley in the 100-mile (160-km) event and Fred Nixon on an Indian was placed in 3rd place.

The 1937 Big Twin Flathead (opposite) featured the new styling of the EL Knucklehead but retained the sidevalve engine configuration. The teak red with black stripes edged in yellow was one of three paint schemes offered that year. The others were delphinium blue with teak red stripes and bronze with delphinium blue stripes edged in yellow. The double loop frame and tubular forks were new for this year, too. The engine (left) now featured dry sump lubrication, the oil feed pump being a vane type, driven from the rear exhaust cam gear shaft, which is when Harley's VL became the UL. The timing case cover (below right) was shaped to assist movement of the crankcase air-oil mist to the new slinger on the generator drive gear and the vane-type pump was relocated to the rear of the cover. The tank-mounted dash (below left) was fitted to the UL as part of the overall redesign.

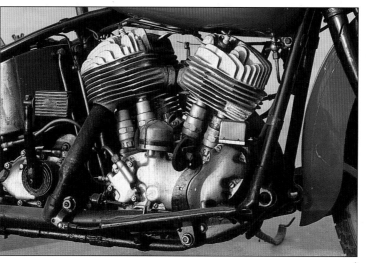

Pages 62-63
Harley-Davidson was one of only two manufacturers to survive World War II and the only one to continue to successfully produce new models. The K models (page 62) were the first of the post-war Sportster line designed to compete with British imports, while the Evolution (page 63) was the engine that saved Harley-Davidson after its return to private ownership in the eighties. It is seen here fitted to a Heritage Softail model.

A 1917 Henderson Four (below) – the first generator model – that formerly belonged to Steve McQueen and is now owned by Lonnie Isam of Competition Motorcycles. The Henderson company was bought by Ignatz Schwinn in 1918 and production was moved from Detroit to Chicago. The Schwinn-produced Henderson Four (opposite) is unrestored but running and was on display at a Florida AMCA meet in March 1997. Owners of such machines have to face the dilemma of whether to restore them to their original condition or retain them in their present, rather weathered, form.

HENDERSON

The company was founded in Detroit by the Henderson brothers, William G. and Thomas W. who came from an automotive background as their father manufactured Henderson cars. Thomas was the President and William the Vice President, the company's designer and engineer. The first Henderson motorcycle to go into production in the 1160 Cass Avenue, Detroit, Michigan factory was made as a prototype in 1911. It featured an in-line four-cylinder engine fitted into what appeared to be an elongated bicycle-type frame. The

machine was equipped with a long cylindrical fuel tank that ran horizontally between the frame tubes. The engine functions of the first model were controlled by a handlebar twistgrip throttle, a hand clutch and a pair of foot pedals. The company's four-cylinder machines gained a reputation for reliability, durability and for being comfortable bikes to ride because of their minimal vibration.

A rider called Carl Stevens Clancy put 18,000 miles (29,000km) on his Henderson in 1913 when he became the first rider to circle the globe. Stressing the quality of its machines in a 1915 advertisement Henderson claimed: 'We were not

content to build a motorcycle that was merely a delight to ride.' While the motorcycles were good the company did not prosper and in 1917 it was purchased by bicycle manufacturer Ignatz Schwinn who already owned Excelsior. Schwinn retained Tom as General Sales Manager and Bill as Chief Engineer. Following the takeover, the company's assets and equipment were shipped by railroad from Detroit to Chicago, Illinois. In December 1918 Tom resigned his position and went to work in the motorcycle export business; Bill Henderson left Schwinn's employ some time in 1919 and went to work for the Ace company that was intent on producing a four-cylinder machine in Philadelphia. He was killed in a motorcycle accident while testing an Ace Sporting Solo and although the company continued in business for a while after his death it ultimately changed hands several times and was finally acquired by Indian who produced four-cylinder machines based on his designs until the time that America entered World War II.

1931 Henderson Model KJ

The Model K was the first new motorcycle from the Henderson company following its takeover by Schwinn and was designed by Arthur Lemon. It was noticeably updated compared to what had gone before because of the switch to sidevalves rather than inlet-over-exhaust valves. It too was superseded by an even more updated machine in 1929: the Model KJ. It retained the same capacity as the earlier K models but featured a stronger crankshaft assembly. The cycle parts were also redesigned with more modern tanks, a restyled frame being incorporated. Sadly the motorcycle was short-lived because of Schwinn's withdrawal from the motorcycle trade in 1931.

1931 Henderson Model KJ (specification)

Country of Origin	U.S.A.
Capacity	1301cc (79 cu in)
Engine Cycle	Four stroke
Number of Cylinders	Four
Top Speed	100mph (160km/h)
Power	40 bhp
Transmission	Three speed
Frame	Steel tubular

The later Henderson motorcycles, such as the KJ model (above), have differently shaped gas tanks which cover the frame tubes. The new tank was introduced in 1929, midway through that year's sales season. The steering head of the frame was altered and the fenders and engine were redesigned. The four-cylinder engine (opposite below) was upgraded through the use of a new Schebler carburettor and new inlet manifold and the crankshaft was strengthened through the use of a five-bearing crankshaft in place of the three-bearing one. The redesigned gas tanks featured a new instrument panel (opposite above) situated on the tank and included a Corbin speedo, oil pressure gauge and ammeter.

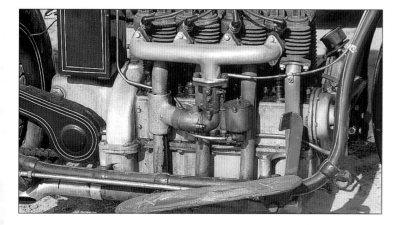

Many consider the last Hendersons, such as the K series model (opposite), to be the best-looking although others would argue that it is simply because they are the most 'modern' in appearance and show the beginnings of the style developed by Harley-Davidson and Indian with, for example, gas tanks that hid frame tubes and sculpted fenders. The two engine types: 1929–31 (top far left) and sidevalve 1920–28 (centre far left) clearly illustrate the cleaner looking later engine. Comprehensive tank-mounted dash (bottom far left) and valanced front fender (left) are from the last Henderson K series machines.

The V-twin Imperial (opposite) is thought to be the only surviving example of a brand of which little is known. It is seen here in its 'as found' condition as it was displayed at Daytona, Florida in March 1997. It is to be renovated by noted vintage motorcycle restorer Pete Bollenbach. The V-twin engine (right) is unusual in that it is a 90° rather than the more common 45° type. More typical of the time it was built is the belt drive, the tubular crossbar between the rail's gas tank and the sprung solo saddle (below).

IMPERIAL

Little is known of the company apart from the fact that motorcycles known as Imperials were made from around 1902 by the American Cycle Manufacturing Company who also marketed some of its machines as 'American' as well as Cleveland, Columbia, Crescent, Eagle, Monarch, Rambler and Tribune, all names used for the pedal bicycles it already made and sold. The company was based in Hartford, Connecticut although early bicycle advertisements indicate that some of these brands were owned by other companies; Crescent Cycles were made by Western Wheel Works and Ramblers by Gormully and Jackson Mfg. and there were also companies such as the American Motorcycle Co. of Chicago, Illinois and the American Motor Co. of Brockton, Massachusetts involved. Imperial is known to have marketed a single-cylinder motorcycle that featured a 4.5 hp engine and a 90° V-twin.

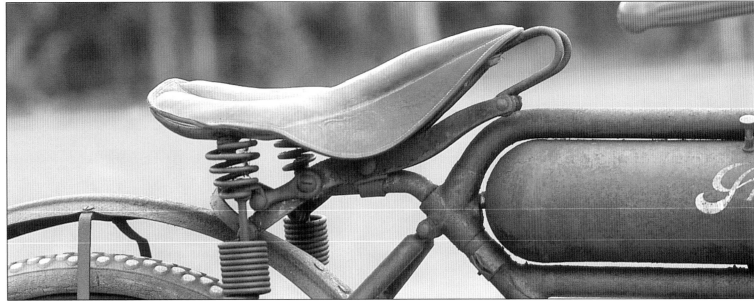

Indian's first motorcycles appeared from 1901 onwards and were known as 'camelbacks' because of the distinctive shape of their tanks, situated over the rear fenders, that held both fuel and oil in separate compartments. The first Indians used small displacement single-cylinder engines (right) that were fitted into the diamond bicycle-type frame in place of much of the seat post. Hendee and Hedstrom, the two men behind the company, had both previously been involved in the cycling industry.

INDIAN

The company was established in Springfield, Massachusetts in 1901 by George Hendee and Oscar Hedstrom who had met through a mutual interest in cycle racing. Their first machine was introduced in the same year and featured inlet-over-exhaust configuration and total loss lubrication that was common in most early machines. This first machine used a bicycle-style diamond frame installed with a single-cylinder engine. Hedstrom designed an engine based on De Dion principles but of a new design using castings that Hedstrom had produced from his own patterns. He also improved the timing and ignition systems and designed a concentric carburettor. The timing was crankshaft-driven and electrical power was supplied by batteries which were carried in a cylindrical tube, fixed to the frame's front downtube. The engine was mounted into a diamond-shaped bicycle-style frame, taking the place of much of the seat post. A fuel and oil tank sat over the rear mudguard, its bottom curved to correspond with the radius: it was divided into two compartments, one for each fluid, and its distinctive shape earned it the nickname 'camelback'. The oil flowed down to the engine through a sight glass, an important feature because of the total loss nature of the lubrication system on the early engines which the rider had to frequently check to see that sufficient oil remained. A small canister-type muffler was bolted under the pedal crank bracket. Control of the engine was by levers mounted on the frame which moved a series of linked rods. One lever operated the throttle while the other advanced and retarded the ignition as required.

In this form, the prototype of what became the first Indian motorcycle was tested by both Hendee and Hedstrom prior to their demonstration to various people, including members of

the press in Springfield. To show off the new motorcycle's capabilities it was ridden up Cross Street Hill where the gradient was approximately one in five. It was duly reported at the time that the new machine started easily and accelerated impressively. The steepness of the gradient proved the theory of all-chain drive as the machine was stopped and started going uphill and immediately showed more promise than the belt-drive machines already in existence. The colour that became famous as Indian red was introduced in 1904 and twin-cylinder motorcycles were introduced in 1907 through use of a V-twin designed by Oscar Hedstrom.

The first machine of 1901 was followed by a small batch of motorcycles and to further promote them Hedstrom rode one around New England velodromes during the intervals between bicycle races. He made circuits at different speeds, demonstrating turns to favourable public reaction. It was possibly because of the duo's European origins that a 1901 Indian was shipped to England in 1902 where it was exhibited at the annual Stanley Bicycle Show which had exhibited motorcycles for a number of years. Once again public reaction was favourable. Hedstrom continued to give practical demonstrations of his machine's abilities, advertising in the bicycling magazines of the day and selling in excess of 140 motorcycles that same year. The upshot of this was that by 1903 Indian was becoming a prominent name within the fledgeling industry. Although Hendee and Hedstrom may have been unaware of the fact, in the same year but in another state William Harley and the Davidson brothers were starting to produce motorcycles in a similarly humble way and the fortunes of the two companies were destined to be forever intertwined. By 1909, Indian had produced a loop frame as pedal and motorcycles diverged. In 1911 Indian had a remarkable success in the Isle of Man TT races when its

George Hendee and Oscar Hedstrom were both immigrants to the United States but named their products, such as this early single, Indian, to indicate that it was a wholly American product. They called their machines motocycles (deliberately leaving out the 'r') as the terminology was not immediately defined and they were seeking to avoid problems with copyright and patent regulations.

The Indians featured precision machine work such as this carburettor of Hedstrom's own design and manufacture (above) and the steering components of the 1914 racer (right).

machines took first, second and third places in that year's senior race.

Special motorcycles were constructed for the TT race which were obliged to conform to the rules and included an anomaly concerning displacement; a maximum displacement of 585cc was permitted for twins while singles were allowed to displace only 500cc because they were considered more reliable. It may not have been strictly true but that was what the rules said. For this race the Indians featured 3.75 hp V-twin engines, each cylinder having a bore and stroke of 70 and

76mm (70 x 76mm x 2 = 585 cc). They also featured chain drive and a two-speed countershaft gearbox. The overall gear ratios were 3.5:1 and 5.08:1 for top and bottom respectively. The racers were designed with a short wheelbase and in order to incorporate the gearbox and engine within this dimension the diameter of the flywheels and crankcase were reduced in diameter. Otherwise, the engines used standard Indian features including overhead inlet valves and side exhaust valves, a mechanical oiling system and detachable cylinder heads. The later components were bolted down with three

Like Harley-Davidson, Indian sought to promote its motorcycles through racing success. This 1914 racer was renovated by California resident Stephen Wright who also restored motorcycles for the late Steve McQueen. It was built for the dangerous world of board-track racing and features an eight-valve engine; in other words, it has two exhaust and two inlet valves per cylinder. It was designed to run full bore with only a cut-out switch used to slow the machine into the turns.

bolts instead of the more usual four and silencers were not required for the race although they were for practice laps before the actual race. An additional oil tank was fitted on the seat tube with a drip feed The tank-mounted gear lever was moved forward and closer to the handlebars so that it could be easily operated from the crouched riding position assumed by racers. The footboards were replaced by pegs which required a modification to the clutch-operating mechanism. The rear brake was footpedal-operated and the twistgrips turned, one to operate the throttle and the other the ignition

advance and retard mechanism.

Charles Franklin was chosen to ride alongside Jake De Rosier as were Jimmy Alexander, Oliver Godfrey and Arthur Moorhouse, all riders acknowledged to be among the cream of the then current road racers. The five-strong Indian team faced severe challenges from more than 50 other bikes including Charlie Collier on a Matchless-JAP single and Frank Phillip on a Scott twin with rotary inlet valves. The race was not a foregone conclusion by any means and much passing and repassing as well as other dramas occurred over the five laps.

This 1914 racer features a hand oiler behind the seat which necessitated the rider taking his hands off the bars and moving a knee at race speeds in order to lubricate the eight-valve V-twin engine (opposite). Ignition was by means of a Bosch magneto controlled by a cut-out switch on the handlebars.

G. S. Davidson watched the race and subsequently recorded what he saw in a book entitled *The Story of the TT*. He noted that the day of the race was bright and sunny presaging that the course would be dry, a distinct advantage when much of the mountain course was farm track, potentially hazardous in wet conditions. Jake De Rosier, dressed in his usual riding attire of running shoes and theatrical tights, took the lead on the first lap. He was trailed by Collier on the Matchless and Oliver Godfrey on one of the Indians. Franklin and Moorhouse were in fourth and sixth places. The other Indian riders were more conservatively dressed in riding breeches, leather jackets and boots. The order changed on the second lap when Collier went into the lead, Godfrey maintaining third place on the Indian with race number 26 despite having stopped for fuel. Jimmy Alexander crashed his Indian (number 7) injuring his knee and damaging the right-hand twistgrip of his machine and Moorhouse moved up to fifth. Things changed again in lap three although Collier extended his lead to almost a minute; but Godfrey passed De Rosier. Further down the field Phillip, reportedly wearing purple leather to match his Scott, made the fastest lap of the day in 44 minutes and 52 seconds but even so was not in the running for the top places. While this was going on Messrs. Franklin and Moorhouse maintained their positions. Lap four saw major changes at the head of the field, Charlie Collier puncturing one of his tyres which caused him to drop back to third place and Jake De Rosier broke down in Ramsey. He spent 20 minutes working on the rear inlet valve and changing a spark plug. Oliver Godfrey, on Indian number 26, meanwhile stepped up the pace and took the lead he had acquired to 2 minutes ahead of Charles Franklin; Arthur Moorhouse on Indian number 31, stayed in fourth place as the racers went into the fifth and final lap. Charlie Collier

mounted another challenge for the lead and passed Franklin, halving the lead that Oliver Godfrey had built up. Despite this, second place was not to be his because he had refuelled away from the official points in Douglas and Ramsey and was consequently disqualified. De Rosier, too, was disqualified after struggling into 11th place because he had fitted a spark plug and a nut that had not been carried on the machine. The top three were Godfrey (26), Franklin (17) and Moorhouse (31) with times of 3.56.10, 3.59.52 and 4.5.34 respectively. The arduous mountain course had taught them numerous lessons: as far as the manufacturers were concerned the single-speed race bike was history as were belt drives. From then on it would be gearboxes and chain drive. The organizers also realized that the differing limits for various engine capacities were unfair so, for 1912, when Franklin and the others would compete again, they introduced flat limits of 500cc for the Senior TT and 350cc for the Junior. Indian naturally made much of its spectacular 1-2-3 victory and it remains to this day the only occasion on which an American-manufactured motorcycle has won an Isle of Man TT race.

Indian survived World War II and produced a huge number of machines for the U.S. Army. In these years Hendee and Hedstrom resigned from the company they had founded having become dissatisfied with the way the board of directors of the company were running it. A new generation of machines followed from employed engineers such as Charles Gustafson who designed the Powerplus which stayed in production albeit sequentially upgraded until 1924. The next generation of motorcycles from Indian were designed by Charles Franklin of which the most notable were the Scout and Chief. These models were introduced in 1920 and 1922 respectively to immediate acclaim. The Chief was initially billed as Big Scout and considered suitable for sidecar work.

Like the smaller displacement Scout the Chief endured for
many years being gradually upgraded and developed –
indeed it was the last American-made Indian to be produced.
During World War II Indian supplied militarized motorcycles
to the U.S. Army, essentially military variants of the Scout
models. During this period they also built an experimental
machine, the 841, for the Army that featured shaft drive, a
transverse V-twin engine and plunger rear suspension. While
it was a successful motorcycle, as was its competitor, Harley-
Davidson's flat twin XA, the Army failed to order either
machine in any great quantity.

1916 Powerplus

Sidevalves had caught on in Europe but only Reading
Standard really developed the idea in the United States under
the direction of Charles Gustafson. He moved to Indian where
he designed a sidevalve engine for the new Powerplus model.
The new design was considerably more powerful than the
earlier ones and was the basis of Indian's success until 1953.

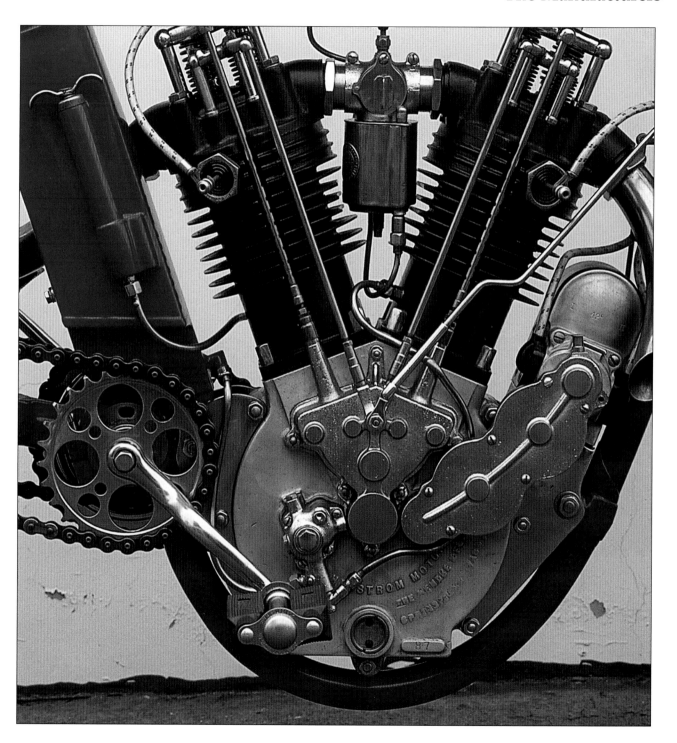

1916 Powerplus (specification)	
Country of Origin	U.S.A.
Capacity	997.6cc (60.88 cu in)
Engine Cycle	Four stroke
Number of Cylinders	Two
Top Speed	60mph (96 km/h)
Power	18 bhp
Transmission	Three speed
Frame	Steel loop

The early racer's primitive engine management checks and rider's controls can be seen in the picture (below left) where the ignition cut-out switch can be seen adjacent to the handgrip on the handlebar end. The wire leading from this switch leads down to the magneto situated forward of the front cylinder (below right). By pressing the switch as the bike approached a turn the rider could cut out the ignition so that the engine would not fire for a few seconds and therefore slow down enough for the rider to make the turn. Also evident here are the valve pushrods, timing cover and oil pump housing.

1917 Model O

Indian was not alone in believing that there was a market for lightweight motorcycles of small displacement. In its range for a number years were lightweight machines including the Model O which was in production between 1917 and 1919. This diminutive motorcycle featured a sidevalve horizontally-opposed twin engine.

1917 Model O (specification)

Country of Origin	*U.S.A.*
Capacity	*257.3cc (15.7 cu in)*
Engine Cycle	*Four stroke*
Number of Cylinders	*Two*
Top Speed	*45mph (72km/h)*
Power	*4 bhp*
Transmission	*Three speed*
Frame	*Steel loop*

1928 Indian Four

The Indian Four was a magnificent motorcycle and its purchase price reflected this. The Four came about as Indian acquired the rights and tooling to the Ace motorcycle when it ceased trading. The first Fours were referred to as Indian Aces although this tag was dropped as Indian's engineers refined the design.

1928 Indian Four (specification)

Country of Origin	*U.S.A.*
Capacity	*1265cc (77.21 cu in)*
Engine Cycle	*Four stroke*
Number of Cylinders	*Four*
Top Speed	*80mph (128kph)*
Power	*30 bhp*
Transmission	*Three speed*
Frame	*Steel loop*

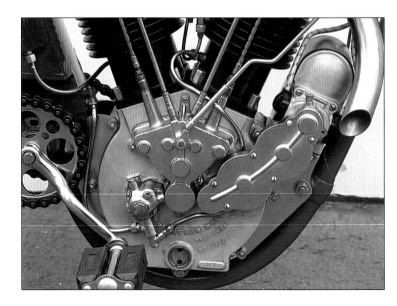

1935 Sport Scout

The Sport Scout was Indian's sports bike brought out in response to the customer and dealer demand for a new model to replace the discontinued 101 Scout. It was introduced in 1934 and had a European look as a result of its girder forks and design of frame that was termed 'keystone' by its makers because of the way it relied on the engine to be part of it. The Sport Scout became the basis of successful Indian racers of the era.

1935 Sport Scout (specification)	
Country of Origin	U.S.A.
Capacity	744cc (45.44 cu in)
Engine Cycle	Four stroke
Number of Cylinders	Two
Top Speed	80mph (129km/h)
Power	25 bhp
Transmission	Three speed
Frame	Keystone steel

1928 101 Scout

Indian Scout reliability became noteworthy and gave rise to the advertising slogan, 'You can't wear out an Indian Scout'. The Scout went through a number of incarnations, all of which brought racing success to the company in its campaigns against arch-rival Harley-Davidson. Many riders felt that the 101 Scout was the best Indian motorcycle made, endowed as it was with handling characteristics that became legendary.

1928 101 Scout (specification)	
Country of Origin	U.S.A.
Capacity	737cc (45 cu in)
Engine Cycle	Four stroke
Number of Cylinders	Two
Top Speed	75mph (121km/h)
Power	18 bhp
Transmission	Three speed
Frame	Steel loop

The overhead valve arrangement of the eight-valve racers can be seen in the picture (below) that illustrates the exposed valve springs for the inlet and exhaust valves on top of each cylinder head.

A 1912 Indian single-cylinder racer (opposite); in this year the Los Angeles one-third-mile Motordrome was opened managed by Paul Derkum, himself a former Indian racer. The Excelsior factory's machines were then ridden by Joe Wolters, Jake De Rosier and Fearless Balke and a week after the opening of the track a crash occurred that eventually led to the death of Jake De Rosier who had formerly been one of Indian's star riders and a member of its Isle of Man TT team. This single-cylinder racer, like the larger capacity V-twins, features overhead valves (above right), magneto ignition (lower right) and an ignition cut-out switch adjacent to the left-hand grip (below left).

1942 Indian 841

This was one of Indian's experimental motorcycles, built by the company at the request of the U.S. Government in the same way that Harley-Davidson built the XA. The 841 had a transverse V-twin engine, shaft drive, girder forks and plunger rear suspension. These features made it a technologically advanced motorcycle for its time but the army failed to order them in significant numbers.

1942 Indian 841 (specification)

Country of Origin	U.S.A.
Capacity	750cc (45 cu in)
Engine Cycle	Four stroke
Number of Cylinders	Two
Top Speed	n/a
Power	n/a
Transmission	Three speed
Frame	Duplex cradle

The Manufacturers

In the years prior to World War II there was renewed interest in motorcycle racing when the AMA introduced Class C, a type of racing for 45-cubic inch V-twins in almost stock form. Both Indian and Harley-Davidson manufactured 45-cubic inch sidevalve V-twins which made for close competition and intense rivalry. Class C racing has survived and the old sidestick bikes still compete under the auspices of organizations such as AHRMA – the American Historic Racing Motorcycle Association. This is Rusty Lowry racing his Indian in Class C at Daytona, Florida during Bikeweek.

Left: Indian did not get as many orders for military bikes as Harley-Davidson as the United States prepared for World War II, but did sell its machines to allied countries including Britain, France and Canada. One of its military machines was the 741-B a 45-cubic inch V-twin: others included the 640-B a 30.50-cubic inch V-twin for the British Army and a number of military Chiefs with and without sidecars.

Left: The 841 was a special motorcycle built for evaluation by the U.S. Army. Based on the requirements of the U.S. Quartermaster, a specification for a cool-running shaft-drive twin was drawn up. Indian produced the 841, a transverse V-twin with shaft drive. Its engine featured some existing Scout parts, but was largely new. In competition, Harley-Davidson produced a flat twin styled after the motorcycles used by the German Army: neither motorcycle was ordered in large quantities.

Right: *Indian had acquired the Philadelphia-based Ace Motor Corporation which produced in-line four-cylinder motorcycles and went on to produce Indian Ace machines and later Indian Fours. The fours were expensive machines to produce and had a limited market so that when World War II arrived production was halted never to be resumed. Indian Fours were included in a batch ordered by the Massachusetts State Police Department which was being assembled when production halted. These 1940 police Indian Fours were, as a result, the last made.*

Opposite: *The big Indian Chiefs, with their hugely valanced fenders, are for many people the epitome of the Indian marque. After World War II, production of the Chief was resumed, using the girder forks designed for the experimental military 841. The Indian factory used bright colours, a legacy of its control by DuPont, on machines such as this 1947 Chief but retained the sidevalve V-twin engine at a time when Harley-Davidson was refining its more modern overhead-valve engine which was proving to be a popular seller.*

This beautifully restored Miller (opposite) dates from 1903 and is typical of early motorcycles; it is powered by a single-cylinder engine (right), driven by a leather drive belt and is constructed around a bicycle-type diamond frame with the oil and fuel tanks suspended from the top tube.

MILLER

Over the years there were numerous small motorcycle companies who quickly came and went during the formative years of the motorcycle industry. Some of these were acquired by other manufacturers, others went out of business, but what they have in common is that little, if anything, is known about many of them because there are no known surviving examples: the only evidence of their existence is the occasional appearance of a yellowing advertisement in an old cycling or motorcycling periodical. It is reasonable to assume that the machines advertised never made it beyond the prototype stage, especially if response to the advertisement was less than overwhelming. There are many estimates of the number of motorcycle manufacturers believed to have existed in the United States, and they vary widely, but it is not exaggerating to say that there have been in excess of 200 during the 20th century. Lists of manufacturer's names do exist and curiously Miller does not appear on any of them.

The Ner-a-Car was an unusual design of motorcycle as demonstrated by this one being ridden at a vintage bike event during Bikeweek in Daytona, Florida. The brand Ner-a-Car was derived from the name of its designer, Carl A. Neracher.

NER-A-CAR

The Ner-a-Car was designed by Carl A. Neracher in America and manufactured from 1921 onwards. The motorcycle had a low-level frame made from steel channel, similar to a car chassis. The machine used a 238cc (14.5 cu in) two-stroke engine that drove the rear wheel through a friction drive. Production was later transferred to England where some models were made with 347cc (21.1 cu in) Blackburne sidevalve engines. Variations made to the Ner-a-Car in its relatively short production run included the fitting of deeply valanced fenders and variations in the front fork design.

PEERLESS

This brand name was used by three different motorcycle companies; two British before World War I and an American company. The American company was based in Boston, Massachusetts and produced machines between 1913 and 1916. They used single and V-twin engines of their own design with Bosch magneto ignition and fitted them into loop frames. Peerless also experimented with shaft drive and telescopic forks. The 1912 5 hp Peerless was a single-cylinder machine with Bosch magneto, a clutch (described as a free engine idler), a gas tank between the frame rails, a sprung saddle and sprung forks.

Pierce was only in business for four years from 1909 to 1913, but during that time produced the innovative Pierce Four (opposite and overleaf) which had what has been described as a T-head layout in which the inverted inlet and exhaust valves were positioned on either side of the four-cylinder engine block (below). Separate camshafts were required to operate each set of valves. The Pierce Four was the first successful shaft-drive motorcycle sold in the United States. The first Pierce Fours did not feature a clutch but later ones had a clutch and two-speed transmission.

PIERCE

Pierce was originally known as the Pierce Cycle Company and was based at 51 Hanover Street, Buffalo, New York. It later became known as Pierce Arrow, was among the pioneers of American motorcycling and also made cars. A Pacific Coast branch of the company was based in Oakland, California. The company produced motorcycles between 1909 and 1913 which included belt-drive singles and a sidevalve in-line four-cylinder machine which had shaft drive. The four displaced 598cc (36.5 cu in). The top tube of the frame was of large diameter and carried the fuel. A clutch and two-speed gearbox

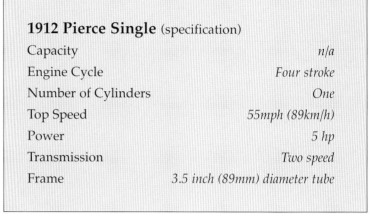

1912 Pierce Single (specification)

Capacity	*n/a*
Engine Cycle	*Four stroke*
Number of Cylinders	*One*
Top Speed	*55mph (89km/h)*
Power	*5 hp*
Transmission	*Two speed*
Frame	*3.5 inch (89mm) diameter tube*

was introduced in 1910.

The Pierce Single featured large diameter tubes which doubled as containers for fuel and lubricant although it was still of the diamond bicycle-type design. The engine featured roller bearings, magneto ignition, mechanically actuated valves and an automatic carb.

In 1912, the Pierce single-cylinder model was powered by a 5 hp motor that featured roller bearings, mechanical valves, an automatic carburettor and magneto ignition. The machine was capable of 55mph (89km/h). The frame of this model, while of the diamond bicycle-style type, was unusual in that its tubing was 3.5 inches (89mm) in diameter and doubled as tanks for oil and fuel. Pierce was proud of the fact that its machines had won eight endurance contests and a Grand Prix in Buenos Aires, Argentina.

Opposite: *To open the Panama Pacific Exposition of 1915 in San Francisco, a group of riders on Pope motorcycles rode from Washington, D.C. to San Francisco carrying the President's proclamation that the exposition was open. A 1915 Model L twin and a single-cylinder machine went the full distance.*

POPE

This early motorcycle company was named after its founder, Colonel Albert A. Pope, who built cars and bicycles as well as motorcycles between 1911 and 1918. For a time the factory was at 502 Capitol Ave, Hartford, Connecticut and later at 16 Cycle Street, Westfield, Massachusetts. The 1912 Pope used a 426cc (26 cu in) single-cylinder engine and retailed at $165 with magneto ignition. The company's advertising of the time stressed that the company had been in business for 35 years and that 'Pope quality has never been questioned'. The firm later went on to produce V-twins as well as singles. The 1914 model displaced 998cc (60.9 cu in) and featured overhead valves. For 1915 the models were listed at $275 and $230 for the twin and single respectively. Front suspension by means of a leaf spring and rear suspension by sprung axle was considered noteworthy as was the two-speed transmission and these features were stressed in the advertising of Pope's range of six motorcycles which were being produced alongside a range of 92 pedal bicycles.

The 1913 L Model Pope motorcycle has the unusual distinction of being immortalized by the U.S. Post Office. On 10 October 1983 a 5 cent stamp was issued that featured a drawing of it by Walter Brooks of Norwalk, Connecticut. The motorcycle had originally been purchased new by John R. Beattie in 1913 and after using it for eight years he placed it in storage where it remained until it was donated to the Smithsonian Museum in 1964.

The Model L was powered by a 7–8 hp V-twin engine with a bore and stroke of 3.328 x 3.5 inches respectively. This amounts to a capacity of 61 cubic inches (1000cc). The cylinders were made from high grade grey iron and had separately cast cylinder heads. The components were bored

and ground to size and relied on external fins for cooling. The valves were mechanically operated and made of chrome nickel steel; they were interchangeable and located in the cylinder heads. The exhaust valve could be lifted to reduce compression in order to ease starting. Care was paid to the design of the internals of the engine: the camshaft was made of nickel steel and the pistons were ground and featured oil grooves to ensure sufficient lubrication. The con rods were made of forged nickel steel and the flywheel was turned and balanced. Phosphor bronze was used for the bearings and the Bosch magneto drive-shaft was mounted in roller bearings. A lever-operated clutch disengaged drive which was by means of a Renold roller chain. The pedal and engine drive chains were interchangeable. A Schebler carburettor was installed, lubrication was by means of a worm-driven mechanical oiler and an auxiliary hand pump was also fitted. The oil level could be checked by a sight glass located in the crankcase.

The frame was the bicycle-style diamond shape although the front downtube was curved and described as a 'keystone' type. The frame was made from 1.25-inch (32-mm) heavy gauge tube and the top tube sloped downwards to ensure a sufficiently low saddle position. The forks were leaf sprung with four leaves in the spring. Rear suspension was also of a spring design, the coiled springs being mounted over the rear wheel spindle to allow some up and down movement over bumps. The machine rolled on wheels of 28 inches (71cm) in diameter although in the early days diameters quoted included the tyres so were in actual fact the overall diameter of the wheel and tyre. Wheelbase was $56\frac{1}{2}$ inches (144cm) and ground clearance $5\frac{1}{2}$ inches (14cm) – this latter measurement then being important because of the poor condition of roads outside towns.

The gas tank was mounted between the two parallel rails

of the frame but designed so that they were not visible. The oil tank was positioned between the seat post and the rear fender. The handlebars were of a tubular tiller design and on them were mounted controls which enabled the right twistgrip to control the throttle while the left lifted the exhaust valve. The ignition control was at the right side of the gas tank. Valanced fenders were fitted front and rear and the Pope came with a luggage rack, a single saddle and a rear stand. The machine was finished in a colour known as Pope Gray and the bright parts were nickel plated.

In 1913 Pope's Model L retailed at $250 while the 5 hp Model M cost $215 and the 4 hp Model K $200. Cheapest of the company's range was the lightweight Model H at $165.

1913 Pope Model L (specification)

Country of Origin	U.S.A.
Capacity	1000cc (61 cu in)
Engine Cycle	Four stroke
Number of Cylinders	Two
Top Speed	n/a
Power	7-8 hp
Transmission	Single speed
Frame	Tubular keystone

The Pope was an innovative machine in its day featuring plunger rear suspension (opposite) and mechanically-operated inlet and exhaust valves made from chrome nickel steel (above) and leaf sprung forks (left) that incorporated quarter elliptic springs.

READING STANDARD

This company flourished in its Water Street, Reading, Pennsylvania factory during the first decades of the 20th century. Its first machines were Thor-engined and not dissimilar to the Indians of the time. Production of both singles and V-twins was carried out with singles of 499cc (30.44 cu in) and V-twins of 990cc and 1170cc. (60.4 and 71.4 cu in). The factory also produced race bikes for professional riders.

In 1907 Reading Standard was the first U.S. manufacturer to build sidevalve engines. These were designed by Charles Gustafson who later moved to Indian where he designed the famous Powerplus engine. In 1908, Reading Standard was claiming to be first to produce the only real mechanical intake valve-equipped motorcycle in the United States and that its machine was the only one to have climbed Pike's Peak, Colorado. Alongside its range of solo two-wheelers the company offered tri-cars, tandems and tricycles. One of the three-wheelers, the tri-car or forecar, was available as a light delivery van; it retailed at $295. The light van body was positioned over the two-wheeled front axle: the axle was fixed to a pair of semi-elliptical leaf springs mounted on a 2-inch (50-mm) section steel channel frame into which was also fitted a 10 hp V-twin engine, a two-speed gearbox and a single rear wheel. Final drive was by means of a chain and steering was accomplished by turning a steering wheel rather than handlebars.

For 1909 the company offered 14 different models including twins and singles ranging from 3.5 to 7 hp with choices of belt or chain drive, battery or magneto ignition, as well as features considered notable at the time, including mechanically-actuated inlet valves and spring forks. Its

advertising of the time trumpeted that there was 'no limit to speed but the law' and pointed out that an owner could expect between 20 and 50 miles (32 and 80km) for 5 cent's worth of gasoline. In 1909 a rider on a Reading Standard achieved a perfect score in the New York to Chicago 1,000-mile (1,600-km) reliability run sanctioned by the Federation of American Motorcyclists (FAM). By 1911 the company was claiming to manufacture the only American motorcycle with an emergency brake in addition to the coaster brake. Reading Standard went out of business in 1922 and was purchased by Cleveland who sold the remaining stock and ceased to use the brand name in 1923.

SEARS

Sears, Roebuck & Co., the Chicago, Illinois-based department store sold motorcycles branded as Sears that were made for it by other concerns at different times in its history. The first time this happened was in 1910 when single-cylinder machines were listed in the company's catalogue.

Sears planned on selling motorcycles from 1908 but as it was a mail order retailer rather than a manufacturer it had to find a company who could supply finished motorcycles in the numbers which it was anticipated Sears could sell. It entered into a contractual arrangement with the Aurora Automatic Machine Company which was the Chicago-based foundry that had been making castings for George Hendee and Oscar Hedstrom for their Indian motorcycles on the understanding that it could sell identical castings to other motorcycle producers once Indian's requirements were met. The Aurora concern did very well supplying Indian who was also prospering, as well as a number of small new companies springing up around the United States. Before the end of the first decade of the 20th

levers. The most extreme divergence from the majority of Thor machines, however, was that the Sears machines also had belt drive. Of Thor's range only one had belt drive, all the others being chain-driven. At this time there was fierce debate within motorcycling as to which method of drive was best because the clutch was yet to be developed. The advantages of a belt were that it could be slipped at junctions allowing the rider to keep the motorcycle engine running, whereas the rider of a chain-drive machine had to switch off the ignition at each stop. Belts were also perceived as quieter-running. The advantage of the chain-drive, though, was that there was no loss of power through slipping and the chain was less susceptible to stretching and therefore lasted longer. A diehard group of motorcyclists favoured belts which is why Thor kept a single model so equipped in their range. Development of the clutch, gearboxes and more powerful engines soon made such concerns of little importance. In the interim though, Sears could sell its belt-drive motorcycle for significantly less than the otherwise similar Thor.

After 1912 the simple single-cylinder machines featured a Spacke single-cylinder inlet-over-exhaust engine with a Bosch

century Indian stopped buying castings from Aurora as the Springfield, Massachusetts company had constructed its own foundry. To replace this business Aurora began manufacturing complete motorcycles under the brand name of Thor from 1908. By 1909 there were nine different Thor models using both single- and twin-cylinder engines. (*See* Thor page 102.)

Sears began to distribute Thor motorcycles under its own label in 1909 and by 1910 there were several differences between these and the Thor bikes. Sears chose to supply their own-brand machines with a British-made Brown & Barlow carburettor and a box was installed behind the seat post to allow the battery, coil and tools to be contained therein. Another difference in detail was that the left twistgrip was used on the Thor to control the ignition advance and the right the throttle but on the Sears version these functions are controlled by handlebar-mounted

1910 Sears Single (specification)

Capacity	*491cc (30 cu in)*
Engine Cycle	*Four stroke*
Number of Cylinders	*One*
Top Speed	*55mph (88.5km/h)*
Power	*4 hp*
Transmission	*Single speed*
Frame	*Steel diamond*

magneto and chain transmission. The entire motorcycle was based around an Excelsior-manufactured loop frame and leaf-sprung trailing link forks. Sears also offered a V-twin-engined machine. Both were dropped in 1916.

Later Sears sold Austrian Puch machines and Italian Gileras as Sears and Allstate brands. It concentrated on lightweights and scooters (some of which were sold as Allstates) but dropped out of motorcycles sales in 1968 as Japanese competition began to get stronger and better organized.

The forks (right above and below) of the Sears single were sprung in an unusual way. The gas tank (opposite above and below) was fitted between the top rails of the frame and had the bracket for the lever that engaged the belt-drive attached to it. As the lever was pushed forwards it tensioned the belt which, through the increased friction, turned the rear wheel. The box below the seat and behind the seat post (below) contained the battery and ignition coil as well as providing space for the toolkit.

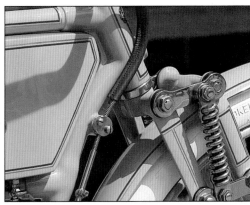

THOR

Thor was the brand name used by the Aurora Automatic Machine Company in the United States. The company manufactured engine castings designed by Indian's Oscar Hedstrom for the Springfield marque. At the time, the company was about to commence manufacture of motorcycles and as part of its agreement with Hendee and Hedstrom used the same castings in its machines. The castings were also supplied to other American manufacturers of the time, including Emblem, Racycle and Reading Standard. Between 1907 and 1919, complete motorcycles were manufactured under the Thor name. There were both Thor singles and V-twins and the company stayed in the motorcycle business – having made both singles and twins – until 1919. The Aurora Automatic Machine Company had its general offices at Thor Building, 1307 Michigan Avenue, Chicago and its sales office and works at 361 West Superior Street in the same city. By 1911 Thor Motorcycles was able to advertise its IV Magneto Model, a single-cylinder-engined model with magneto ignition, and boast that 'Thor Motorcycles won every Endurance contest held last season'.

The 1915 V-twin Thor was known as the model U and rated at 12 horsepower. It utilized an inlet-over-exhaust engine and, according to its makers, offered 'reliability, consistency, speed and power'. The Model U was typical of its time with a diamond-type frame, an angular between-the-rails gas tank, and an angular oil tank behind the seat post and forward of the rear fender. Large rectangular footboards were provided for the rider and the gearshift was on the right-hand side of the gas tank. Other controls were mounted on the handlebars. A sprung solo saddle and rear fender-mounted luggage rack completed the machine. Front and rear fenders and gas and oil tanks were painted and finished with pinstriping around their edges.

The company is known to have used innovative engineering in some aspects of its motorcycles. One such feature was the Aurora fork; this was not dissimilar to a girder fork arrangement in that the suspension relied on the parallelogram arrangement of the fork for the wheel spindle and the portion of the forks fitted to the frame. The up and down movement was dampened by short springs. (This assembly can be seen on the 1910 Sears single on page 98.)

YALE

The Consolidated Manufacturing Company of Toledo, Ohio began motorcycle manufacture at 1702 Fernwood Avenue, Toledo after it acquired an existing California-based company, Yale. Its other products at the time included steel tubing, bent parts and drop forgings. From these beginnings in 1902 it went on to produce both singles and V-twin-engine designs of motorcycles. The single of 1910 displaced 500cc (30.5 cu in) and relied on an atmospheric inlet valve and battery and coil ignition. The machine was ruggedly engineered to withstand travel on the poor roads of the time. In 1910 the company also introduced a 45° V-twin of its own design. The new engine displaced 1000cc (61 cu in) and had mechanical valve actuation. The 1910 V-twin featured two-speed transmission and a clutch mechanism. The two-speed transmission featured constant mesh planetary gears and a multiplate disc clutch. Gear shifting was by means of a hand lever mounted to the left of the gas tank. It had three positions: pulled back towards the rider, low gear was selected; forward one position for neutral; forward another position and high gear was selected. The motorcycle retailed at $285 while the single-cylinder machine, also equipped with the two-speed transmission, was $235. By 1912

the Yale range included 4, 5 and 7 horsepower machines – models 24, 25 and 27 respectively – which ranged in price from $210 to $285. Two versions of the Model 24 were available, the 24 and the 24M, the M suffix indicating a Bosch magneto. Yale motorcycles had within their construction triple anchored handlebars, dual oiling systems, double grip control (of the engine functions) and wide mudguards. This latter item was no doubt an important consideration where the machine would frequently be operated on unsurfaced roads. Production ceased in 1915.

Above and opposite: *The Thor racer dates from 1908 and its frame is clearly inspired by bicycles of the day. The V-twin engine is unusually inclined and was essentially a pair of the same single castings used in Indian singles as Aurora, who made Thor machines and also made castings for Hendee and Hedstrom's Indian company.*

Keeping Them Going

A number of components were manufactured by specialists and supplied to motorcycle manufacturers for the machines they were constructing; this included chain for both primary and final drive applications (right and far right) and carburettors (opposite) from companies such as Heitger, Schebler and Linkert.

From the earliest days motorcycle manufacturers bought in parts to complete their machines: carburettors are an obvious example and specialist companies such as Heitger, Schebler and Linkert all made carburettors for numerous makes of motorcycles. Many other parts were bought in from specialist manufacturers; Bosch magnetos were made in a 206 West 46th Street factory in New York City; Stewart Speedometers were made at 1910 Diversey Boulevard, Chicago and numerous companies offered cyclemotor engines to upgrade pedal cycles into small capacity motorcycles.

Parts that wore out, such as drive chains, were supplied by a variety of companies including Coventry Chains, Herbert F. L. Funke at 112 Broad Street, New York, H.R. Chains by

Peter A. Frasse Inc. at 419 Canal Street, New York and Duckworth Chains by the Duckworth Chain and Manufacturing Co. of Springfield, 'as fitted to 1917 Hendersons' the advertisement announced. Benton spark plugs were made in Vergennes, Vermont while Champion plugs were made in Toledo, Ohio. Tyres are other consumables on motorcycles and companies including Goodyear, Federal, U.S. Tires and Diamond were among those competing for the motorcyclist's custom: 'Watch the list grow', prophesied their advertisement.

For 1912 the Eclipse Machine Co. of Elmira, New York offered clutch assemblies on which they had a patent and supplied units to Merkel, Emblem, and Yale as standard equipment. Wagner, Pierce, M&M, Haverord, Pope, Detroit, Marvel offered them as optional equipment.

Angsten-Kock of 4068 Princeton Avenue, Chicago offered motorcycle locks, the start of what was to become a large aftermarket industry. MECO – Motorcycle Equipment Company of Hammondsport, New York had an accessories

While some companies, including Flying Merkel, used proprietary brand carburettors (below left), Indian used a carburettor of Oscar Hedstrom's own design (below right) although it was later dropped in favour of a proprietary unit to reduce manufacturing costs. Tyres (opposite) were another item made by specialist manufacturers and many of the companies who were among the first suppliers are still in business.

catalogue as early as 1913 that offered 1,216 items. It had been in business nine years and had also established a Pacific Coast branch in Los Angeles. Another company in a similar line of business was the American Thermo-ware Company Inc. with offices at 16–18 Warren Street, New York and 143 N. Wabash Avenue, Chicago. Among its lines were goggles, horns, sirens, mirrors and lamps. Clothing became available specifically designed for motorcyclists and had novel trade-names like Kant Leak suits and Koverauls. The latter were supplied by Nathan Novelty Manufacturing Co. of New York City. Electric lights were an accessory required by many and were marketed by companies such as the Remy Electric Company of Indiana and the Prest-O-Lite Co. of the same state.

The sidecar was a popular addition to many motorcycles at the time, especially for family men. Several manufacturers, including Harley-Davidson and Indian, supplied their own sidecars but specialist manufacturers such as the Flexible Side Car Co. (so-called because it leaned with the motorcycle during cornering), Rogers, Pullman and Goulding prospered. There were also commercial three-wheelers, sidecars with van

bodies, forecars (trikes with two wheels at the front), and later Harley-Davidson and Indian three-wheelers known as the Servi-Car and Dispatch-Tow respectively which were introduced within a year of each other at the beginning of the thirties.

Enthusiasts have been keeping the early American motorcycles going all over the world for longer than their makers could ever have imagined; here Alan Forbes, an Edinburgh Indian dealer, leads the participants in an international Indian rally in Scotland.